WATERLOO to SOUTHAMPTON

by steam

Bruce Oliver

NOODLE BOOKS

ISBN   978-1-906419-14-1

First published in 2009 by Kevin Robertson
under the **NOODLE BOOKS** imprint
PO Box 279
Corhampton
SOUTHAMPTON
SO32 3ZX

www.kevinrobertsonbooks.co.uk

Printed in England by Information Press, Eynsham, Oxford.
www.informationpress.com

Front cover: - 34087 '145 Squadron', here with nameplates removed, leans to the curve through Farnborough Main with the 1.30 p.m. departure from Waterloo to Weymouth. The elegant gantry, towering over the scene, controls movements in the 'up' direction. 34087, built in December 1948, was one of its class to survive until the last month of steam, July 1967. Farnborough Main opened with the extension from Woking Common to Winchfield (Shapley Heath) in 1838 but the present station buildings date from the 1903 reconstruction. As with other stations along the route, the centre island platform, serving the fast lines, has been removed. 19 August 1966.

Preceding page: - At Waterloo, platform 13, Standard 3MT 82006 stands at the buffers, released from stock brought in from Clapham yard. New in May 1952, 82006 was withdrawn in September 1966. Platform 13 was renumbered 15 when the road between platform 11 and the original platform 12 was taken for the insertion of new platforms (12 and 13). Waterloo had opened for traffic in 1848, with major rebuilding spanning the years 1903 to 1922, the link to Waterloo Jct. on the S.E.R. disconnected during this period. 26 June 1966.

(All photographs by the author.)

CONTENTS

Above - *A mildly hectic scene on platform 10 at Waterloo, where 35008 'Orient Line' has recently arrived on a train presumably from Weymouth (the 1130?). The scene is enlivened by reminders of the time, B.R.U.T.E. trolleys with mail bags, a refreshment attendant preparing for the next 'down' service, luggage handling at the open doors of a Bulleid BCK and passengers moving here and there. Meanwhile, it seems BOAC are urging us to take a trip to Nassau by BOAC at 3.15 p.m. on a Friday afternoon. 7 July 1967*

Opposite - *34001 'Exeter' is here heading a special, via Havant, to the city after which it is named. It stands in platform 11 at Waterloo whilst a 'Warship' waits in platform 9 on a timetabled service to Exeter. Electric traction completes the scene where, in platform 7, a 2BIL heads an Alton line service. 34001, new in June 1945 and rebuilt in November 1957, was withdrawn from service on the last day of steam in July 1967. 8 January 1966.*

WATERLOO to SOUTHAMPTON

The railway line that runs between London and Southampton evolved in a number of stages during the years when railway mania was gripping the country, the 1830s and 1840s.

The original London terminus for the London & Southampton Railway opened at Nine Elms on 19 May 1838. Ten years later, on 11 July 1848, by which time the London & South Western Railway had been established, a new terminus at Waterloo opened, the original terminus complex continuing as a freight depot for the next century and beyond. The 1838 opening took the line from Nine Elms to Woking Common, a temporary terminus until the next temporary terminus took over on 24 September 1838 at Shapley Heath, later to become Winchfield. The extension to Basingstoke followed in 1839, where the station opened on 10 June that year. The next advance took the form of an out-of-order continuation, inasmuch as the section between Winchester and Southampton (Terminus), which also opened on 10 June 1839, preceded the opening of that between Basingstoke and Winchester by nearly a year, the latter taking place on 11 May 1840. The line that was to continue west, turning right at Southampton Junction for Blechynden (Southampton West from July 1858), came much later, opening on 29 July 1847. Quadrupling of the L.& S.W.R. main line had been completed through to Worting Junction by 1909.

Electrification of the route extended over many decades, with piecemeal openings to meet the needs of an increasing commuter market. Waterloo to Clapham Jct. and beyond was partially electrified between October 1915 and January 1916 for suburban services to East Putney, Wimbledon and Strawberry Hill, together with an extension to Hampton Court Junction, to serve Hampton Court and Claygate. Electrification from Hampton Court Junction to Woking Junction came in January 1937, in connection with the scheme serving Guildford, Portsmouth and Alton. Electrification from Sturt Lane onwards to Southampton occurred thirty years later, in July 1967, when steam motive power was finally eliminated from the region. Southampton Terminus, the original station serving Southampton, was closed for passenger use later the same year.

The following pictures cover ground already well trodden by countless photographers in the pursuit of steam during the final few years. As subject material, they are therefore conspicuously unoriginal

in concept, though each captures a moment that will not have featured in any previous book. (However, about twenty individual pictures have, over the years, been reproduced in the historical magazine, Back Track).

The collection is a personal archive, one that I am pleased to be able to bring to a wider audience as a contribution to the story of the final years of steam on the line to Southampton. Whilst the photographs might be considered fairly routine, I hope they offer sufficient variety and richness of interest, featuring locomotives that were inevitably neglected and shabby at the time, living out their last few years in a state of ambivalent regard. They may have been despised by officialdom but they were revered by those in pursuit, perhaps out of all proportion to the service they gave - a case of economics versus romanticism.

By 1963, traditional Southern steam locomotives had all but vanished from the scene, following the mass withdrawals of 1962, leaving behind a squadron of survivors of later construction, viz. Bulleid Pacifics, Standard classes and Ivatt tank engines.

During the final years, here illustrated, Bulleid Pacifics suffered the gross indignity of identity loss, with nameplates and smokebox number plates removed as the months passed, reinforcing the mise en scène of the day, neglect, terminal decline and dereliction. Filth abounded, a far, far cry from earlier days, particularly those prior to WWI, when railways commanded the respect of the nation and appearances mattered, a time when steam locomotives symbolized pride and self-esteem.

Regrettably, colour photography of railways in the 1960s was fraught with impending disappointment, the occupational hazard of low film speed too often imposing severe restrictions where moving subjects were concerned. Present day practice bears no comparison, with film speed eight times better – and digital! – offering opportunities that were denied to those embarking upon photography in the 1960s. Admittedly, there will be found here striking differences in picture quality. Certain images have been included for no reason other than the fact they are part of the same portfolio, rather than for any intrinsic merit. However, if some of the pictures contained herein manage to fill a few gaps in an already well-documented archive on the subject, the exercise will, I hope, have been worthwhile.

Bruce Oliver. Southsea 2009.

Above - *On a murky October afternoon, 34088 "213 Squadron', awaits departure from platform 10 at Waterloo on the 4.35 p.m. departure. In platform 8, a service from Portsmouth has just arrived with a 4BUF as the rear unit. 8 October 1966.*

Opposite - *Ivatt 2MT 41319 and Standard 4MT 80015 await their next carriage duties, standing in one of the two 'vestigial' platforms that came between platform 11 and the original platform 12, since extended to form the present day platforms 12 and 13. Delivered new in May 1952, 41319 lasted until the very end in July 1967 - as did 80015, a locomotive that pre-dated 41319 by some seven months, in October 1951. 3 July 1967*

BIBLIOGRAPHY

The following published works have been consulted:

BRITISH RAILWAY STEAM LOCOMOTIVES 1948-1968,   Hugh Longworth. OPC 2005.
PSL FIELD GUIDE - RAILWAYS OF THE SOUTHERN REGION,   Geoffrey Body. Cambridge 1984.
HISTORY OF THE SOUTHERN RAILWAY,   C F Dendy-Marshall, revised by R W Kidner Ian Allan 1968.
RAILWAY TRACK DIAGRAMS, Part 5 - ENGLAND SOUTH AND LONDON UNDERGROUND.
   Quail Map Company 2002.

Above - *34041 'Wilton', a locomotive that had performed on the S.& D.J.R. quite often, waits on the coal road, with a Standard 3MT beyond. Launched in September 1946, 34041 lasted until January 1966. Its record of service was relatively undistinguished (inasmuch as it was only beaten into bottom place by 34091'Weymouth'), averaging just 2,605 miles per month throughout its career. (34006 'Bude' came out best with 4,244 m.p.m.)*

Top left - *Five studies of Nine Elms motive power depot, from October 1965 - still 21 months before the final curtain - announce, undeniably, the end of an era, with desolation and decay influencing the scene. (1) 34024 'Tamar Valley' and Standard 4MT 76069, both alive - if scarcely kicking - are here found on a shed road, looking towards the turntable. 34024, delivered new in February 1946, had been rebuilt in February 1961. It was one that lasted until July 1967. 76069's life lasted from August 1956 until June 1967. 10 October 1965.*

Lower left - *35005 'Canadian Pacific' is photographed on the very day it was withdrawn from service. Entering service in January 1942, 35005 had been rebuilt in May 1959. 35005 held - and holds! - the undistinguished record of being the least active member of its class in service, achieving an average of only 3,427 miles per month. At the other end of the table, 35025 'Brocklebank Line' achieved 4,653 miles per month, 36% better! Having since completed many hours of service in main line preservation, 35005 has somewhat made amends.*

Overleaf - *Alongside one of the buildings at Nine Elms stand four locomotives, side by side. From left to right, they are 34004 'Yeovil' (June 1945 - July 1967), 34048 'Crediton' (November 1946 - March 1966), 34088 '213 Squadron' (December 1948 - March 1967) and 75069 (September 1955 - September 1966 - subsequently preserved). 34004/48/88 had been rebuilt in February 1958, March 1959 and April 1960, respectively.*

Above - A bleaker scene it would be hard to imagine - weeds and dereliction join Standard 3MT 82027 in a picture of a depot in terminal decline. 'Wilton' is glimpsed poignantly through the line of life-expired water cranes. 82027 was delivered new in November 1954 and lasted in service until January 1966. It had, here, not long to go. 10 October 1965.

Opposite top - A dirty scene at Clapham Jct., as 35012 passes on an 'up' train. The famous gantry signal box still had many years to go but not before suffering a partial collapse on the northern side. 35012 'United States Line', while retaining its nameplates, is here in a very sorry external condition. Rebuilt in February 1957, 35012's life spanned the years from January 1945 until April 1967. The London & Southampton Railway had opened its 'Wandsworth' station in 1838, since which time Clapham Jct. has evolved as a junction of some distinction. 24 October 1965.

Opposite lower - 34012 'Launceston' is seen at Clapham Jct., platform 8, on the 1.12 p.m. from Bournemouth. It had then not long been deprived of its nameplates. Rebuilt in January 1958, 34012 dated from October 1945 and was withdrawn from service in December 1966. Also seen In the picture are a Standard 3MT and a diesel shunter. 24 October 1965

Above - 34013 'Okehampton' gathers speed through Wimbledon on a 4.40 p.m. boat train to Southampton Eastern Docks. Note that the stock includes examples of three liveries - green, maroon and the then new blue/grey. Rebuilt in October 1957, 34013 entered service in October 1945 and lasted until the very end, in July 1967. Wimbledon station had opened with the Nine Elms to Woking Common scheme on 21 May 1838. April 1967.

Opposite - 34104 'Bere Alston' seems to be going well - through Raynes Park, powering the 3.30 p.m. from Waterloo to Weymouth. 34104 was delivered new in April 1950, rebuilt in May 1961 and condemned in June 1967. 12 March 1965.

Raynes Park is here host to 34021 'Dartmoor', rushing past a 4SUB on the slow (platform) line. Its train is the 6.22 p.m. Waterloo-Bournemouth. 34021's dates run from January 1946 to July 1967, rebuilt in December 1957. Raynes Park opened in 1871 on the site of Epsom Jct., which dated from the 1859 Epsom line development. April 1967

Above - 35010 'Blue Star' is found travelling light engine through Surbiton, interestingly having lost its smokebox plate but not its nameplates! The code indicates a journey from Nine Elms to Southampton Terminus but one can speculate whether this be an accurate description. 35010 emerged in July 1942, was rebuilt in January 1957 and lasted in service until September 1966. Surbiton opened with the main line in 1838 but has since seen considerable development. It was resited in 1845 and then extensively modernised in 1936-39. 2 April 1965.

Opposite top - 73083 was one of the original batch of ten Standard 5MT locomotives delivered to the Southern (Eastern Section) when new in July 1955. It was withdrawn in September 1966. It is here seen coming through Raynes Park on the 3.35 p.m. from Waterloo to Bournemouth West, going along a treat. 12 March 1965.

Opposite lower - Regarded as an interloper on the Southern, 73092 was one of the many Standard 5MT exiles that appeared during the final years of steam. 73092 is here bound for Clapham yard on a mixed train of vehicles and is seen passing Berrylands - a station with little other than a couple of platforms to offer the passenger. 73092, new in October 1955, lasted in service until July 1967, another of the final loyal band. Berrylands had opened for suburban services on 16 October 1933, in response to local housing development. 10 October 1965.

Above - *Taken shortly after the picture of 35010, 34057 'Biggin Hill', carrying the same code, is almost certainly bound, as the description suggests, for Southampton Terminus. It is therefore possible that 35010 was replaced by 34057 on this train and that 35010 was unwell. 34057, 'born' in March 1947, 'died' in May 1967.*

Opposite top - *34098 'Templecombe' drifts nonchalantly through Esher on the 5.22 p.m. departure from Waterloo, bound for Bournemouth. It fails completely to attract the gaze of waiting passengers, which is a shame. The tall signal gantry is a commanding structure, while the platform offers a taste of Southern style, with concrete lamp standards carrying characteristic hexagonal glass shades. Rebuilt in February 1961, 34098 had been delivered new in December 1949 and lasted in service until June 1967, not quite making it to the end. Esher, one of the original 1838 stations, had carried the names Ditton Marsh, Esher & Hampton Court and Esher & Claremont. 19 August 1966.*

Opposite lower - *34009 'Lyme Regis', new in September 1949 and rebuilt in January 1961, heads for Salisbury on the 5.41 p.m. departure from Waterloo. It is seen passing Hersham, where the Southern lamp shades retain their frames - unlike those at Esher q.v. 34009 here had just six weeks to go, being condemned in October 1966. The station at Hersham dates only from 1936, when platforms were provided for the slow (suburban) lines. 19 August 1966.*

Above - One of the exiled Standard 5MT locomotives, 73002, passes Walton-on-Thames on the 6.09 p.m. departure from Waterloo, bound for Basingstoke. 73002, new in May 1951, ran in service until March 1967. Walton-on-Thames is another of the original stations on the 1838 line to Woking Common, later widened to four tracks. 19 August 1966.

Opposite top - On a misty March afternoon, 35011 'General Steam Navigation' makes its way through Walton-on-Thames on the 3.30 p.m. departure from Waterloo. 35011 emerged in December 1944 and remained in service until February 1966, having been rebuilt in July 1959. 35011 still exists, if as a somewhat long-term project. 2 April 1965.

Opposite lower - Framed lamp shades still adorned Walton-on-Thames when 34053 'Sir Keith Park' passed by on the 5.23 p.m. Waterloo departure for Bournemouth. 34053, completed in January 1947, was rebuilt in November 1958. Withdrawn from service in October 1965, 34053 survives as the focus of a preservation project. 2 April 1965.

Overleaf - Weybridge station is cavernous and offered a dramatic setting for passing steam trains. Here 73083, its history outlined in another caption, passes on the 3.35 p.m. departure from Waterloo for Bournemouth. Weybridge station is another dating from the line's opening in 1838. The branch to Chertsey opened in 1848, with the extension to Virginia Water following in 1866. Electrification arrived in 1937. 19 August 1966.

MANN&Cº ESTAT
AGENT

73083

ESTATE AGENTS

RUGBY & CHARD

WALTON ON THAMES

Opposite top - *At West Byfleet, the 'down' fast and slow lines embrace an island platform. On this occasion, 34102 'Lapford' speeds on its way to Bournemouth with the 3.30 p.m. departure from Waterloo. 34102 began its career in March 1950, one of very few built at Eastleigh, and, like so many of its class-mates, opened its account on the Eastern section. It came to Bournemouth in 1958, continuing in service through to the last rites of July 1967.West Byfleet did not open with the line to Woking Common in 1838, coming into being 49 years later in 1887. 18 August 1966.*

Opposite lower - *At Woking, S15 30833 leaves by the 'up' fast line on a stopping service from Basingstoke to Waterloo. This locomotive was completed in November 1927 and gave service until May 1965, representing value for money. As Woking Common, the station opened on 19 May 1838. The present station is a tribute to the Southern Railway's bold dedication to 'concrete modernism' and dates from 1938. 20 September 1963.*

Above - *Entering Woking is 34056 'Croydon' on the 5.30 p.m. departure from Waterloo. Apparently still well-maintained externally, 34056 lasted another nine months until May 1967. Built in February 1947 and rebuilt in December 1960, it was one of the top dozen performers in its class, recording an average of 3,938 miles per month. 16 August 1966.*

Opposite top - *An unusual view of Woking, taken from parcels' bay, finds 34025 'Whimple' entering the 'down' fast platform, on the 1030 a.m. departure from Waterloo for Weymouth. 34025 entered traffic in March 1946, was rebuilt in October 1957 and came through to the last weeks of steam in July 1967. 17 August 1966.*

Opposite lower - *A low evening sun catches 35014 'Nederland Line' emerging from the shadows of Woking's canopies. The train is the 6.30 p.m. from Waterloo to Weymouth. 35014 was completed in February 1945 and lasted until March 1967. It had been rebuilt in July 1956. Southern faceted lampshades here retain their metal ribs. 26 August 1966.*

Above - *A potentially busy scene faces the photographer at Woking, where S15 30512 enters platform 1 from the sidings, the code suggesting a journey to Feltham in the near future. In the distance, an 'up' boat train from Southampton Western Docks approaches, while another S15 stands in the sidings. 30512 had been built 42 years earlier in February 1921 by the L.& S.W.R. and was to last in service another six months. 20 September 1963.*

Overleaf - *Passing the sub-station at Woking Jct. is 34054 'Lord Beaverbrook' on a stopping train to Salisbury. The yard at the time was always very busy, invariably overflowing with engineering wagons, a function it has retained over the decades, if since rationalized. 34054 emerged into service in January 1947 and survived until September 1964. It here has just one year to go. The Guildford branch at this point had opened in 1845. 20 September 1963.*

Opposite top - On a stopping service from Salisbury is 34092 'City of Wells', here found about to enter St.John's cutting on the outskirts of Woking. 34092 eventually entered main line service in preservation, having been withdrawn from capital stock in November 1964. It had been new in September 1949. The line west of Woking Common had opened on 24 September 1838 as far as Winchfield, then known as Shapley Heath. 20 September 1963.

Opposite lower - The 1.30 p.m. from Waterloo makes fine progress through St.John's cutting, Woking, with 35021 'New Zealand Line' in charge. 35021 dated from September 1948 and was rebuilt in June 1959. It lasted in service until August 1965. 20 September 1963.

Above - Coming through St.John's cutting, Woking, is 73118, hauling a Brighton line 6PAN unit to Eastleigh works. 73118 was an original South Western Division Standard 5MT and, at one time, had carried the name 'King Leodegrance', continuing the memory of 30739. 73118 was a 'final act' performer, lasting until July 1967. It had been delivered new in December 1955. 20 September 1963.

Overleaf - En route from Feltham, bearing the code for Southampton Docks is 33040, the last member of Class Q1. 33040 had been delivered into service in December 1942, the entire class of forty locomotives having taken only nine months to be constructed. 33040 was condemned in June 1964. 20 September 1963.

Opposite top - 35028 'Clan Line' sails effortlessly through Brookwood on the 4.35 p.m. from Waterloo, the train name 'Royal Wessex' no longer carried. 35028 needs no introduction, more famous in main line preservation, perhaps, than ever it was in day-to-day service. Delivered new in December 1948, it was rebuilt in October 1959. Brookwood will always be associated with the London Necropolis & Mausoleum Company and its cemetery on the south side of the station, from which a point a branch was constructed into the grounds in 1854. On the north side of the station, a bay platform, dating from 1890, had served Bisley rifle ranges. The Bisley branch closed in 1952, while the Necropolis branch had done so a decde earlier in 1941. 16 August 1966.

Opposite lower - Standard 4MT 76018 approaches Brookwood on the 'down' slow line with an engineering train. 76018 was one of the original 4MT deliveries from Horwich to the Southern Region in July 1953. It was withdrawn from service in October 1966. 18 August 1966

Above - 35012 'United States Line' negotiates the cutting just east of Farnborough and is about to pass beneath the Basingstoke Canal. The train is the 3.30 p.m. service from Waterloo to Bournemouth and Weymouth. 30 May 1966.

Above - 73113 brings the 3.35 p.m. from Waterloo under the Basigstoke Canal aqueduct. 73113, one of the original South Western division 5MT allocation, was delivered new from Doncaster in October 1955, surviving until January 1967. It had carried the name 'Lyonnesse', bequeathed by 30743 (condemned in October 1955). 30 May 1966.

Opposite top - Emerging from beneath the substantial footbridge (glazed and enclosed) at Farnborough Main, 34056 'Croydon' rushes round the bend with the 1.30 p.m. from Waterloo to Weymouth - nameplate and crest in evidence. 18 August 1966.

Opposite lower - To the west of Farnborough Main station, the 'down' gantry frames the 'Bournemouth Belle' as it passes on its way to Bournemouth with 34100 'Appledore' in charge, a Pacific still in fine condition - externally at least. 34100, new in December 1949, was yet another to last until the final weeks of operation in 1967. It had also been at the centre of events during the final weeks of steam on the former South Eastern main line. 18 August 1966.

Opposite top - Between Farnborough Main and Fleet, 35010 'Blue Star' strides along - apparently without exhaust - en route to Weymouth with the 1.30 p.m. from Waterloo. 30 May 1966.

Opposite lower - The lower quadrant gantry controlling the 'up' lines at Fleet offers two clear roads, while 35030 'Elder Dempster Lines' travels in the opposite direction on the 4.35 p.m. from Waterloo to Weymouth, the service that originally carried the name "The Royal Wessex'. 35030, delivered in April 1949, was condemned in July 1967. It had been rebuilt in April 1958. Fleet opened in 1847 - as Fleetpond - but the present station is a total rebuild, dating from the architecturally - and aesthetically - barren years of the mid-1960s. 15 August 1966.

Above- In commendably clean external condition, 34005 'Barnstaple' coasts through Fleet under the lower quadrant gantry controlling the 'down' direction lines. The train is the 1.25 p.m. from Weymouth. 34005 emerged new from Brighton Works in July 1945. It was rebuilt in June 1957 but only lasted another two months after this picture was taken, succumbing to withdrawal in October 1966 - external condition here being, perhaps, deceptive. 15 August 1966.

Opposite top - The 5.30 p.m. departure from Waterloo drifts through Winchfield station, en route to Bournemouth. 35027 'Port Line' is in charge, sadly shewing signs of considerable neglect. 35027 had entered service in December 1948. It was rebuilt in May 1957 but did not make it to 'the end', having been withdrawn in September 1966. However, it is one of ten of the class to have survived into preservation as a working example. Known as Shapley Heath at the line's opening in 1838, Winchfield had, by this time, long since lost its island platform. 15 August 1966.

Opposite lower - Winchfield station is here host to 34013 'Okehampton', hauling the 6.00 p.m. ex-Waterloo, bound for Salisbury. Standard upper quadrant signals are here in place on the 'up' side gantry. 15 August 1966.

Above - Standard 5MT 73086 approaches Winchfield with the 11.10 a.m. from Bournemouth to Waterloo. Delivered new from Derby in September 1955, 73086 began its career on the Eastern Division. It had carried the name 'The Green Knight', the former identity of 30754 (condemned in February 1953). It was itself condemned in October 1966. 30 May 1966.

Above - *About to pass beneath 'Suicide Bridge', Winchfield, is 35003 'Royal Mail', here devoid of nameplates. It is in charge of the 9.21 a.m. from Weymouth to Waterloo. 35003, new in September 1941, was rebuilt in August 1959 and survived in service until the last week of steam in July 1967. 30 May 1966.*

Opposite - *34077 '603 Squadron' brings the ' Bournemouth Belle' under the tall bridge that attracted the title 'Suicide Bridge', just west of Winchfield station. Though in deplorable external condition, 34077 does, at least, retain symbols of identity, nameplates and smokebox number plate. It had been delivered new in July 1948 and was to last until March 1967. Rebuilding had taken place in July 1960. 30 May 1966*

Opposite top - Approaching Basingstoke and passing the closed signal box at Barton Mill is 76054, assisting D6536, which had failed. The train is a Waterloo-Basingstoke service. New from Doncaster in April 1955, 76054 continued in service until October 1964. The extension from Winchfield (Shapley Heath) to Basingstoke took place in 1839, contemporaneous with the opening of the line between Winchester and Southampton, leaving only the section from Basingstoke to Winchester to be opened a year later, in 1840. The G.W.R. route from Reading came into being eight years later, in 1848, while the branch to Alton did not open until 1901. 11 July 1964.

Opposite lower - 34095 'Brentor' reaches Basingstoke on the 1.30 p.m. from Waterloo, with a long way still to go. 34095 was delivered new in October 1949 - from Eastleigh, rather than from Brighton. Rebuilt in January 1961, it went on until the very end, July 1967. 16 August 1966.

Above - 34100 'Appledore', looking good, accelerates towards Basingstoke station after pause for thought, while operating the 1.30 p.m. from Waterloo to Weymouth. 17 August 1966.

Opposite top - *35012 'United States Line' takes the 9.24 a.m. from Bournemouth away from Basingstoke - a rake of green vehicles, apart from the inclusion of one maroon specimen. The new white signal box is a striking feature, situated in the fork between the former L.& S.W.R. and G.W.R. lines. 30 May 1966.*

Opposite lower - *34023 'Blackmore Vale' approaches the junction at Basingstoke with the 1.30 p.m. from Waterloo, here seen overtaking a freight on the slow line, with a D65xx (Class 33) in charge. 34023, new in February 1946, passed quickly into preservation upon withdrawal in July 1967. 10 September 1966.*

Above - *Making an unusually fierce noise for a Bulleid Pacific, 34047 'Callington' storms away from Basingstoke with the 12.59 p.m. from Bournemouth to Waterloo, a six-coach train, generously augmented by vans. 34047 had entered service in November 1946. It emerged from rebuilding in November 1958 but did not make it until the very end, being withdrawn in June 1967. 16 August 1966.*

Above - *31408 takes a rest at Basingstoke, while engineering staff gather strength for the afternoon shift. 31408 had been built at Ashford in 1933, entering service in September that year. It survived until June 1966, just three months after this scene was caught on camera. 20 March 1966.*

Opposite top - *30824 glides into Basingstoke on the 3.54 p.m. stopping train from Waterloo. 30824 had been built at Eastleigh in March 1927; it enjoyed quite a long life, retiring in September 1965. 11 July 1964.*

Opposite lower - *30838 brings a freight, bound for the Salisbury direction, through the slow line platform at Basingstoke. 30838 emerged new from Eastleigh works in May 1936 and was withdrawn from service in September 1965. It is coupled to a flat-sided bogie tender. 25 July 1964.*

Above - About to turn left on to former Great Western territory is 45132 on the Bournemouth-York service. In the final years of steam on the Southern, Stanier Class 5 locomotives were not infrequent visitors, bringing a welcome element of variety to the scene. Note the Stanier vehicle next to the tender. 19 August 1966.

Opposite top - Entering Basingstoke from the west is 73088, carrying an improvised smokebox number plate. 73088 began its working life on the Southern on the Eastern section, following delivery from Derby in September 1955. It was withdrawn from service in October 1966. It had carried the name 'Joyous Gard', in memory of 30741.73088 is here in charge of a boat train from Southampton Western Docks and is bound for Waterloo. The structure in the right background is Basingstoke motive power depot. 16 August 1966.

Opposite lower - On the 'down' fast line, 35012 'United States Line' waits to leave Basingstoke for Bournemouth on an inter-regional combination, the 10.25 a.m. from Manchester Piccadilly and the 10.05 a.m. from Liverpool Lime Street. 11 July 1964.

Pages 54-55 - A Class 4MT (76xxx) waits in the down slow line at Basingstoke on a stopping service, silhouetted against the setting sun. March 1967

Pages 56-57 - 34042 'Dorchester' is about to continue south from Basingstoke on an inter-regional service, while 31401 has arrived alongside on a stopping service from Waterloo. 34042 still carries the headcode 'M02' which was that for the northbound working the same day, the locomotive travelling as far as Oxford. 34042 was new in October 1946, its condition here suggesting it might have lasted longer than it did, succumbing to withdrawal in October 1965. It had been rebuilt in January 1959. 31401, released new from Ashford in August 1932, was condemned three months earlier than 34042, in July 1965. 11 July 1964.

34066 'Spitfire', fully recovered from its memorable mishap at Lewisham, is about to depart Basingstoke and is thought to be bound for Portsmouth on an inter-regional service, a conjecture open to question. 34066, though necessarily confined to works in February and March 1958 following its misfortune, was not rebuilt. It was eventually withdrawn from capital stock in September 1966. 11 September 1966.

Above - *A photograph taken from the trackbed of Thorneycroft's Siding, the extant stump of the former branch line from Basingstoke to Alton. Standard 4MT 80065 is travelling light engine, carrying the code for Feltham to Eastleigh or Southampton, though this claim may here be misleading. 80065 was new from Brighton in September 1953 and lasted in service until September 1966. The line to Alton lasted only from 1901 to 1936. 10 September 1966.*

Opposite - *An unusual light engine movement takes 34104 'Bere Alston' past Battledown, with the falling gradient of the 'up' line from the flyover as a backdrop. The line to Andover was opened in 1854 and extended to Salisbury in 1857. 21 August 1965.*

Pages 62-63 - *The peace of the evening is shattered alongside the 'up' distant near Steventon, as 35028 'Clan Line' stampedes past, in great style, on the 6.30 p.m. from Waterloo to Weymouth. 30 May 1966.*

Opposite top - *The rising gradient taking the 'up' Bournemouth line through the flyover at Battledown is here crossed by a public right of way. 73110 is found hauling a train of vans in the 'down' direction. Doncaster-built in October 1955, 73110 had carried the name 'The Red Knight', the former identity of N15 30755, which ran in service until May 1957. Thus, an overlap of about 19 months existed between their careers. 73110, the first of ten Standard 5MT locomotives delivered new to the South Western division, was withdrawn in January 1967. 29 May 1966.*

Opposite lower - *35013 'Blue Funnel' pauses at the distant signal near Steventon, while working the 6.05 p.m. Whit Monday extra from Bournemouth to Waterloo. 30 May 1966.*

Above - *A bonfire sends particles skywards in the background as 76067 drifts through Micheldever on a train of vans bound for Portsmouth & Southsea. 76067 emerged new from Doncaster in August 1957 and was to see service on the Southern for a month under a decade - i.e. until July 1967, the very end. Micheldever has, for a station so remote, a building of some distinction. 16 August 1966.*

Opposite top - 35028 'Clan Line' yet again, this time streaking through Micheldever on the 4.35 p.m. departure from Waterloo to Weymouth - no longer bearing the headboard 'The Royal Wessex'. 17 August 1966.

Opposite lower - The 3.35 p.m. from Waterloo to Bournemouth comes under the road bridge at Micheldever. 34026 'Yes Tor' is in charge, with only a month to go before being withdrawn in September 1966. 34026, new in service in April 1946, was rebuilt in February 1958. 17 August 1966.

Above - The 10.30 a.m. departure from Waterloo, bound for Weymouth, descends from Wallers Ash tunnel in the charge of 34017 'Ilfracombe'. New in December 1945, 34017 was rebuilt in November 1957 and withdrawn from service in October 1966. 29 May 1966.

Above - *34108 'Wincanton' at Worthy just south of Winchester Jct., working the 0933 from Waterloo to Bournemouth. 34108, new in Aril 1950, was rebuilt in April 1961, only to be condemned six years later, in June 1967. The author's mother here intrudes upon the scene, never one to be denied the chance to study a steam train. 29 May 1966.*

Opposite top - *34004 'Yeovil' passes former Winchester Jct., where the branch to Alton once diverged to the north east. It is here seen hauling the 1.30 p.m. from Waterloo to Weymouth. 21 October 1964.*

Opposite lower - *Winchester City is here host to 35013 'Blue Funnel', about to depart for Waterloo on the 3.10 p.m. from Bournemouth. Winchester had first been served by trains from the south, until the Basingstoke connection was completed in 1840, a year later. The branch from Alton, joining at Winchester Jct., opened in 1865. 31 August 1965.*

Above - *The 'up' approach to Winchester City was - and is - characterised by a deep cutting, crossed by a trio of high bridges. In this picture, 34012 'Launceston' tackles the long drag to Micheldever with the 9.21 a.m. departure from Weymouth, bound for Waterloo. The enamel running in board provides an emphatic Southern image. 1 September 1965.*

Opposite top - *The approach to Shawford invariably produced fast running. Here, 34002 'Salisbury' makes the most of the favourable gradient with a spirited display on the 8.35 a.m. departure from Waterloo. 34002 made its debut. in June 1945, going on to serve the South Western division throughout its life - until April 1967. Had 34002 made it to the very end, it would surely have entered preservation, as the earliest surviving 'non-rebuilt'. Shawford station opened in 1882, over four decades after the line itself, in 1839. 16 August 1966.*

Opposite lower - *A quaint mixture of oddments is brought south through Shawford by Standard 4MT 76064, a locomotive delivered new from Doncaster in July 1956 and one that served the region until the final weeks in July 1967. 15 August 1966.*

Opposite top - *To the south of Shawford, 34086 '219 Squadron' brings the 'Bournemouth Belle' towards Eastleigh, here thought to be deputising for a Merchant Navy at the last minute. 34086 emerged new - in apple green livery - in December 1948. A capital stock item until June 1966, it had led a busy life - in both the east and the west. 30 August 1965.*

Opposite lower - *With Shawford station as a backdrop, 34056 'Croydon' climbs northwards with the 9.21 a.m. from Weymouth to Waterloo. Shawford's platform canopies, if architecturally undistinguished, were quite sufficient. In the foreground is seen a single track, that formerly used by G.W.R. trains, from Newbury and Didcot. 15 August 1966.*

Above - *Taken from a passing train, 30839 brings a freight towards Eastleigh and Southampton. 30839 had been despatched new from Eastleigh works in May 1936, remaining in service until September 1965. 27 August 1965.*

Above - *35008 'Orient Line' approaches Allbrook, to the north of Eastleigh yard, hauling the 1.30 p.m. from Waterloo. 35008, new in June 1942, had been rebuilt in May 1957. It was one of those that saw out steam in July 1967. 24 April 1965.*

Opposite top - *At the junction with the line to Romsey, 34040 'Crewkerne' approaches Eastleigh station with the southbound 'Pines Express' from Manchester. The signal box at the junction had but a few months to go before demolition, while 34040 laboured on until July 1967. It had been built in September1946 - and was rebuilt in October 1960. Eastleigh had opened as Bishopstoke in 1839, with the line between Southampton and Winchester, the line to Fareham and Gosport forming a junction in 1841. Renamed Eastleigh & Bishopstoke in 1889, a carriage works was opened nearby in 1891. The new locomotive works opened in 1909, in the fork of the two lines to the south, when engineering transferred from Nine Elms. The 'up' island platform is no longer an island. 1 September 1965.*

Opposite lower - *6980 'Llanrumney Hall' coasts into Eastleigh station on a van train. Though devoid of nameplates, 6980 here manages to look dignified and fit for duty. It was to remain in service a further 16 months, until October 1965.It had been delivered new from Swindon just prior to nationalization, in November 1947. 29 June 1964.*

Overleaf - *34064 'Fighter Command', Giesl ejecter fitted in April 1962, passes Eastleigh station with the 'Cunarder' boat train, here carrying the route code for Waterloo to Southampton Western docks. 34064 emerged new in July 1947 and was withdrawn in May 1966. 2 July 1964.*

Opposite top - 35012 'United States Line' is here using the 'down' through line at Eastleigh station, while in charge of the 2.30 p.m. from Waterloo to Weymouth. There is here, as yet, no sign of the new signal box to the left. 14 August 1965.

Opposite lower - 35027 'Port Line', here seen four days after the Winchfield view, is still carrying its number chalked on the buffer beam. On this occasion, at Eastleigh station, the train is the 10.30 a.m. from Waterloo to Weymouth. 19 August 1966.

Above - Looking towards the Romsey line from the 'down' island platform at Eastleigh, 34033 'Chard' is found working the 8.37 a.m. from Bournemouth West to Waterloo. 34033, delivered into service in June 1946, remained in capital stock until December 1965. 30 April 1965.

Opposite top - *Taken from the 'down' island platform, 35022 'Holland-America Line enters Eastleigh on a company special for an opening ceremony at the Pirelli General factory, nearby. 30 April 1965.*

Opposite lower - *31816 hits bright early morning sunshine as it takes the outer platform face on the 'down' side with a van train for Southampton Terminus. 31816 left Ashford works brand new in January 1922 and survived in use for 44 years, succumbing to withdrawal in January 1966, just days after this photograph was taken. 3 January 1966.*

Above - *Coming off the line from Romsey, 34019 'Bideford' brings a train of cement wagons into Eastleigh, bearing the headcode for Waterloo to Bournemouth. 34019, brand new in December 1945, survived until March 1967. 14 August 1965.*

Above - *The signal box at the junction with the line to Romsey at Eastleigh is here in the very process of demolition, as 35003 'Royal Mail' passes by, its own consignment to demolition just five months away. The train is the 1.30 p.m. departure from Waterloo. Note the new signal box to the left of the picture. 10 February 1967.*

Opposite top - *73037 makes its way through Eastleigh station, on a train of vegetable products from Southampton Docks and is bound for Nine Elms. 73037, another displaced exile, emerged from Derby in September 1953 and served the Southern during its own final years, until the end of steam in July 1967. April 1967.*

Opposite lower - *The south end of Eastleigh station witnesses the passage of 34047 'Callington', working the 2.22 p.m. from Waterloo to Bournemouth. 14 August 1965.*

Above - 31800 stands at the outer face of the 'down' island platform at Eastleigh, with a service to Southampton Terminus. Bulleid set 838, here recently repainted, unusually has green gangway ends. 31800, delivered new from Ashford in December 1928, was withdrawn from service in October 1965. 28 April 1965.

Opposite top - 34019 'Bideford' is here seen passing Eastleigh, employed on the 12.35 p.m. from Waterloo to Weymouth. 11 September 1965.

Opposite lower - 34086 '219 Squadron', awaits departure from Eastleigh on the 5.20 p.m. to Fratton. The departure time of this stopping service to Portsmouth varied by a few minutes over the years, a service principally serving the needs of employees at the nearby railway workshops. 28 April 1965.

Overleaf - 34015 'Exmouth' gathers speed through Eastleigh after a signal check, with the 8.35 a.m. departure from Waterloo. 34015 had been a November 1945 delivery; it did not make it until the end of steam, withdrawal from service coming in April 1967. 30 August 1965.

Above - *80152 is here towing 31639, 31408 and 73114, the trio on a final journey to the scrapyard, while 80152 itself, delivered new in February 1957, lasted another 11 months, until July 1967. 31639, the last 'U' to be built at Ashford, started life in May 1931 and was withdrawn in June 1966. [Details for 31408 appear in the Basingstoke picture.] Standard 5MT 73114 had been a Doncaster built of November 1955, one of the original South Western division allocation, lasting until June 1966. 30751's memory had been perpetuated during the years when 73114 carried the name 'Etarre'. 19 August 1966.*

Opposite top - *South of Eastleigh station, the works entrance and the Portsmouth line (originally to Fareham and Gosport, opened 29 November 1841) diverge from the main line to Southampton. With a Hampshire diesel unit forming a backdrop, 34103 'Calstock' glides past on the 'Pines Express', a named train then recently transferred from the S.& D.J.R. route. 34103, new in service in February 1950, was withdrawn in September 1965. 29 June 1964.*

Opposite lower - *30834 comes past the works at Eastleigh - shortly after the previous picture was taken - working a van train to Southampton Terminus. 30834, new from Eastleigh works in November 1927, lasted until November 1964. 29 June 1964.*

Above - *Taken from the same vantage point as the previous two pictures - Campbell Road, Eastleigh - Ivatt 2MT 41313 is found hauling a freight of considerable weight towards Southampton Eastern Docks. 41313 survives in preservation, having been delivered new from Crewe in 1952. It was withdrawn in November 1965. 11 September 1965.*

Opposite top - *Rounding the curve at Swaythling is 34061 '73 Squadron' on the 2 p.m. departure from Eastleigh, bound for Bournemouth West. 34061 entered active service in April 1947 and is here seen during its last full month in capital stock, withdrawal following in August 1964. 2 July 1964.*

Opposite lower - *73117 drifts towards St.Denys, with a boat train for Southampton Western Docks. 73117, new from Doncaster in November 1955, was one of the original ten Standard 5MT locomotives allocated to the South Western division. It had carried the name 'Vivien' for several years, recalling 30748, an N15 withdrawn from service in November 1955. 73117 was withdrawn in March 1967. St.Denys opened in 1861 with the branch to Netley coming five years later in 1866, a line that was extended to Fareham in 1889. 1 September 1965.*

Overleaf - *34019 'Bideford' makes strong statement as it comes past Eastleigh m.p.d. with a Warwickshire Railway Society tour special. 5 September 1965.*

Above - *34060 '25 Squadron' guides a boat train to Southampton Eastern Docks through St.Denys, past a barley-twist gas lamppost on the island platform. 34060, new in service in April 1947, survived until June 1967. It had been rebuilt in March 1960. 19 August 1966.*

Opposite top - *Standard 4MT 80015 comes north through St.Denys with an empty stock working from Poole to Eastleigh. 1 September 1965.*

Opposite lower - *South of the junction with the line from Netley, 34002 'Salisbury' passes St.Denys while working the 8.35 a.m. from Waterloo. 18 August 1966.*

Opposite top - *Ivatt 2MT 41294 travels with its precious load, comprising a single bogie van of L.M.S. design, towards the junction at St. Denys. New from Crewe in October 1951, 41294 was condemned in September 1966. 18 August 1966.*

Opposite lower - *A somewhat murky scene at Mount Pleasant crossing, complete with stylish signal box, as 34090 'Sir Eustace Missenden' passes with the 11.18 a.m. from Weymouth to Waterloo. The leading Standard BSK is already in the new corporate image of blue and grey. 34090 had been delivered new in February 1949 and was another locomotive to make it to the very end of steam in July 1967. Rebuilding had taken place in August 1960. 7 January 1967.*

Above - *Approaching Bevois yard, Standard 5MT 73155 brings an Eastern Docks boat train through St.Denys. 73155 was one of many such migrants to find use on the Southern towards the end of steam. 73155 had been built at Doncaster, emerging in December 1956 and was to continue in service until the last weeks, in July 1967. 18 August 1966.*

Page 98, top - *Standard 5MT 73110 stands at Southampton Terminus, the original end-of-the-line when train services were inaugurated between Nine Elms and Southampton in 1840. The station closed in September 1966 - 10 months before the final rites for steam traction - and just six days after this photograph was taken. 31 August 1965.*

Page 98, lower - *The street facade of Southampton Terminus station, with a representative sample of road vehicles for 1966 on display in the forecourt. The suffix 'Terminus' had replaced 'Town for Docks' in July 1923. 31 August 1966.*

Page 99, top - *The crossing at Canute Road, leading to the Docks, is adjacent to Terminus station. Standard 4MT 76026 is here holding up road traffic as it carefully negotiates the route, the disc code indicating a journey from Nine Elms via Brentford, Chertsey and Woking. 76026, new from Doncaster in November 1953, lasted in service until the final curtain in July 1967. 31 August 1965.*

Page 99, lower - *At No. 3 Gate, Southampton Docks, USA 30067 ponders the next move. 30067, built in 1942, transferred to the Southern (Region) in July 1948, specifically for use in Southampton Docks. It was withdrawn in July 1967. 2 September 1965.*

Above - *Emerging from the tunnel is 35017 'Belgian Marine' on the 11.30 a.m. from Waterloo. 35017 emerged new from Eastleigh works in April 1945, three weeks before the end of World War II. Rebuilt in March 1957, 35017 continued in service until July 1966, a year before the end of steam. 14 August 1965.*

Opposite top - *35016 'Elders Fyffes' bears down upon Southampton Central powering the 10.30 a.m. from Waterloo. 35016 was outshopped new in March 1945 and rebuilt in April 1957. It was withdrawn from service almost two years before the end of steam operation - in August 1965. Southampton Central evolved in stages, following the opening of the line from Southampton Jct. to Blechynden in 1847. Blechendyn was retitled Southampton West in 1858. A new, resited, station opened as Southampton West in 1892, at which time the elegant clock tower with ogee domed roof was built, only to be cruelly destroyed for the 1967 electrification scheme, at a time when architectural barbarism raged nationwide, sweeping away so many elegant buildings. The third (5-platform) station was completed in 1935, when the title Southampton Central became established. In more recent times, the suffix 'Central' had been dropped, only to be reinstated some years later. 24 July 1965.*

Opposite lower - *Taken from the same position as the previous picture, 34075 '264 Squadron' is ex-works from Eastleigh, here found working the 11.16 a.m. from Bournemouth West to Newcastle-upon-Tyne. 34075 was put into service in June 1948 but lasted only until June 1964, when, as a BR(WR) locomotive, it suffered the consequences of being in the spiteful hands of Western Region management - during the regime of Mr Stanley Raymond. 4 August 1962.*

Pages 102-103 - 34036 'Westward Ho' and 35028 'Clan Line', stand side by side in the 'up' platforms at Southampton Central. 35028 is here working the 12.20 p.m. from Bournemouth to Waterloo. 34036 had been built in July 1946, with rebuilding coming fourteen years later in August 1960. Withdrawal in July 1967 was inevitable. 13 August 1966.

Opposite top - Standing at the London end of platform 1, 34071 waits to leave Southampton Central with a Channel Islands boat train from Weymouth. 34071 '601 Squadron' had been the first of a new build, to be delivered after nationalization in 1948. It had, therefore, known no identity other than '34071'. It was rebuilt in May 1960 and lasted in capital stock until April 1967. 29 August 1964.

Opposite lower - 34016 'Bodmin' arrives in Southampton Central with the Bournemouth - York service. 34016 arrived on the scene in November 1945, rebuilding coming in April 1958. Saved from demolition, 34016 survives in preservation and has, to its credit, performed splendidly on main line specials in more recent times. 19 October 1963.

Above - An end-of-platform scene of activity, as 35019 'French Line C.G.T.' receives attention before proceeding to Bournemouth from Southampton Central. Meanwhile, Standard 4MT 76061 goes on ahead with a service from Portsmouth to Bristol or Cardiff. 35019, new in June 1945, was rebuilt in May 1959 and went on to serve the Southern until withdrawal in September 1965. 76061, a Doncaster product of June 1955, was withdrawn in January 1967. 24 April 1964.

Above - *30857 'Lord Howe' brings the 10.25 a.m. Poole to Bradford into Southampton Central. 30857 was, at this time, living its last few weeks of active service, withdrawal coming one month later in September 1962. It had been delivered new from Eastleigh works in December 1928. A splendid collection of L.M.S. stock is here on show. 4 August 1962.*

Opposite top - *Southampton Central's imposing brick signal box stood at the west end of platform 1. Here, it is being passed by USA DS233. Formerly 30061 and built in 1942, it had entered service with the BR(SR) in May 1951. It was one of that celebrated bunch of locomotives to have made it through to the last weeks of steam in July 1967. 20 August 1966.*

Opposite lower - *34044 'Woolacombe' stands at the signal gantry that controlled the western exit from Southampton Central. It is here working the 9.30 a.m. from Waterloo on the shortest day of the year, in blazing low sunshine. 34044 emerged new in October 1946, was rebuilt in May 1960 and continued in capital stock until May 1967. 21 December 1965.*

Above - *En route to the United States for exhibition is 60008 'Dwight D. Eisenhower', here being towed to the Docks through Southampton Central - appropriately by 35012 'United States Line'. New in September 1937, 60008 was withdrawn from service in July 1963. 24 April 1964.*

Opposite top - *Making its way westwards is 34021 'Dartmoor', with the civic buildings and the station clock tower visible as a backdrop. The train is the 11.30 a.m. from Waterloo to Bournemouth West. 24 July 1965.*

Opposite lower - *With Southampton Central's iconic clock tower in the background, 35029 'Ellerman Lines' makes a move from platform 4 with the 12.35 p.m. departure from Waterloo. 35029 entered traffic in February 1949 and was rebuilt in September 1959. Upon withdrawal in September 1966, it eventually made its way to the scrapyard of Woodham Bros. in Barry but was reprieved in 1974, to be sectioned for exhibition at the National Railway Museum in York. 28 August 1966.*

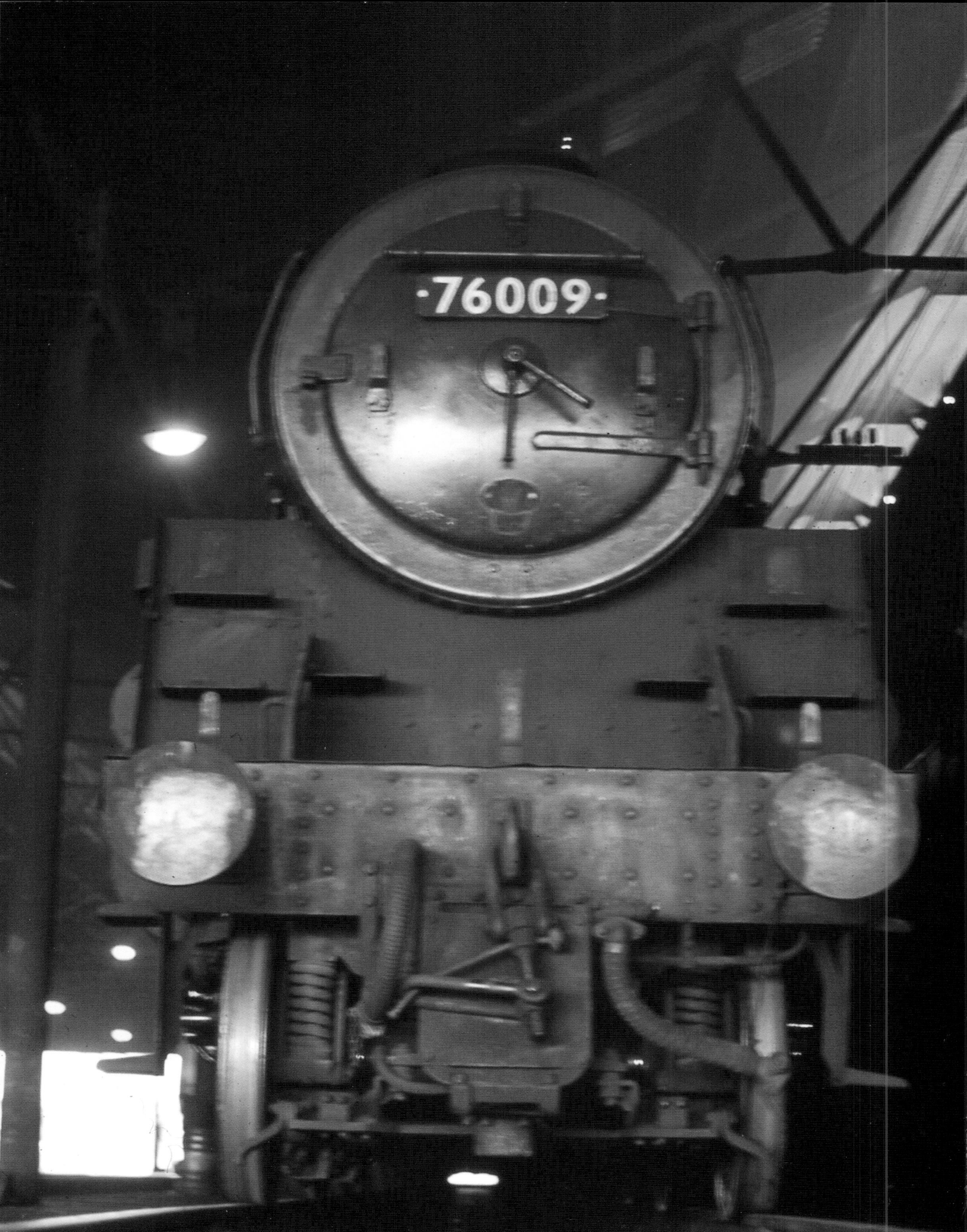
76009

Above - *S15 30834 is here undergoing major overhaul in the Works. March 1964*

Opposite - *Standard 4MT 76009 stands over the pits inside the m.p.d. Condemned in July 1967, 76009 had begun life, new from Horwich works, in February 1953. 5 September 1965.*

Page 112, top - *34055 'Fighter Command' is a forlorn sight, standing outside the front of the Works. It had been withdrawn in June 1963 with a failed middle cylinder but went on for a while, providing steam for safety valve testing. Its smokebox door is here replaced by that from 34043 'Combe Martin', the latter having been condemned during the same month. 34055 and 34043 were new in service in February 1947 and October 1946, respectively. 7 September 1963.*

Page 112, bottom - *35026 'Lamport & Holt Line' and 34005 'Barnstaple' in the test bay outside the front entrance to the Works. 35026, new in December 1948 and rebuilt in January 1957, was withdrawn in March 1967. 6 November 1965.*

Above - *Freshly painted, 34052 'Lord Dowding' stands outside the rear of the m.p.d. 34052 emerged from works in December 1946 and was rebuilt in September 1958. It was one of those that lasted until the end in July 1967. 7 March 1964.*

Page 114, top *- U 31628 stands at the rear entrance to the depot, its external appearance belying the fact it had been withdrawn from service three months earlier, in June 1964. 31628 had been Ashford-built in April 1929. 12 September 1964.*

Page 114, bottom *- N 31831 stands outside the rear of the depot, with another two years' work ahead in capital stock. It was Ashford-built in July 1924 and was 'signed-off' in April 1965.*

Page 115, top - *N 31865, here awaits imminent disposal. Condemned in September 1963, it was to be dealt with a few days after the photograph was taken. 31865 had been built at Ashford in June 1925. 7 March 1964.*

Page 115, bottom - *S15 30500 is here parked at the rear of the m.p.d., withdrawal coming two months later, in June 1963. 30500 dated from May 1920. April 1963.*

Opposite top - *34041 'Wilton', 34079 '141 Squadron', 5MT 73016 and Q1 33006 stand in line at the rear of the m.p.d., dates of withdrawal being January, February, December and January 1966 respectively. 34079, 73016 and 33006 had first reported for duty in July 1948, September 1951 and June 1942, respectively. 20 March 1966.*

Opposite lower - *K 32338 lives out its final hours, still largely intact, at the rear of the Works. 32338 had been built at Brighton in December 1913. 7 September 1963.*

Above - *Life expired and awaiting the final call is H16 30517, withdrawn five months earlier in November 1962. It had been built at Eastleigh, entering service in November 1921. H16s used to operate cross-London freights but ended their days on Fawley branch workings. April 1963.*

Pages 118-119 - *M7 30053 silhouetted against the evening sun, stands at the front of the m.p.d. It had been withdrawn 22 months earlier and here awaits preparation for despatch to North America. Happily, it later returned home and now, operating in preservation, delights all who come to be charmed by its personality. 20 march 1966.*

Opposite top - Q1 33020 stands alongside the coaling plant. New in May 1942, 33020 lasted until January 1966. 14 April 1964.

Opposite lower - Q1 33018 had already been condemned two months previously, in July 1965, when this picture was taken. It awaits disposal in a line of engines, all having suffered the same ultimate fate. 33018 dated from April 1942. 11 September 1965.

Above - '700' class locomotives 30697 and 30700 stand nearest the camera in a line of condemned engines on the south side of the m.p.d. 30697 and 30700 had been delivered new into service in April and May 1897, respectively; both were withdrawn from capital stock in November 1962, over 65 years later. 7 March 1964.

Opposite top - O2 30225, withdrawn in December 1962, stands in a line of condemned locomotives, sandwiched between a USA and an M7, 30328. 30225 had emerged new from Nine Elms in November 1892. April 1962.

Opposite lower - The first of the Southern's delivery of diesel shunters, 15201stands at the back of the m.p.d., withdrawn from service. 11 September 1965.

Above - Looking very much the worse for exposure to the elements, USA 30070 waits its turn to be prepared for further use, as departmental DS238. Withdraw initially in October 1962, it survived in departmental use until August 1963. It survives in preservation. April 1963,

Opposite top - *B4 30096 stands at the rear of the m.p.d., a few weeks prior to its withdrawal in October 1963. It had been built at Nine Elms in November 1893. Following withdrawal, it undertook a period of industrial use before moving into preservation. It had, at one time, carried the name 'Normandy'. 30089 (November 1892 - March 1963), of the same class, is glimpsed in the background. It, too, had once carried a name - 'Trouville'. 7 September 1963.*

Opposite lower - *A1 DS680 here rests on one of the lines at the front of the Works, withdrawn from Lancing Carriage Works in June 1962. DS680 had begun life in February 1876 as LB&SCR 54 'Waddon', later renumbered 654. In 1932 it was renumbered by the Southern Railway as 680S, later DS680, when it took up employment at Lancing. It was later restored at Eastleigh as 54 'Waddon' for public display in Canada. April 1963.*

Above - *USA 30069 deals with Hastings diesel unit 1019 at Eastleigh Carriage Works. In the background is one of the then new BRCW diesel locomotives, later Class 33. 30069, built in 1943, was withdrawn in July 1967. 3 July 1963.*

Page 126, top- *S1236S, here seen sandwiched between Bulleid and Standard Mk.I vehicles, was a Maunsell 8-compartment second class carriage, part of Eastleigh batch 1130-1280, dating from 1930-34. It would almost certainly have disappeared from service very shortly after this appearance. 24 April 1964.*

Page 126, bottom - *DS70133, a former brake vehicle began life as L&SWR 'Ironclad' 1357. It was later renumbered 3193 by the Southern Railway and probably converted to Departmental duty in about 1962. Initially, it had formed part of L&SWR 5-car set 7c, later SR 437. Brake vehicles in this class were 'handed', 3193 having its corridor on the left side; 3192, its set partner, would have been right-handed. It is here seen near Eastleigh Carriage Works. 3 July 1963.*

Page 127, top - *DS136 was new as SE&CR 1247 in August 1913, renumbered by the Southern Railway as 3511 in April 1926. It had been a constituent of set 606, moving to departmental use in January 1958 as DS3511 initially. It was repainted, as seen here in April 1964 in olive green. Originally this vehicle provided brake, second and third class accommodation, the second downgraded to third in about 1926. 20 April 1964.*

Page 127, bottom - *DS1had been built in 1885, as L&SWR inspection saloon 21s, later entitled 'Directors' Saloon'. Renumbered as 1s by the Southern Railway, it retained this identity until about 1950, when it is thought to have acquired the 'DS' prefix. The underframe was renewed in about 1950. It saw a period of use as an instruction vehicle for motormen, during electrification in Kent, 1959-61. 3 July 1963.*